The Book of Care

Compassionate
Action
Restoring
Energy

A little book celebrating healing and wellbeing

DeAnna LoCoco

The Book of CARE
Copyright © 2016
DeAnna LoCoco
Published by Crystal Pointe Media Inc.
ISBN: 978-1-7322673-5-0

All rights reserved. No part of this book may be reproduced or transmitted in any form or by any means, electronic or mechanical, including photocopying, recording, or by any information storage and retrieval system, without permission in writing from the author at: ahdeanna@sbcglobal.net

DISCLAIMER
The contents of this publication are intended for educational and informative use only. They are not to be considered directive nor as a guide to self-diagnosis or self-treatment. Before embarking on any therapeutic regimen, it is absolutely essential that you consult with and obtain the approval of your personal physician or health care provider.

Cover Design by Linda Manzella

Dedication

*To the healing hands and hearts of all caregivers -
celebrating the Art of Healing…*

Unfoldment

Welcome to the world of Energy and its healing power!

Life Itself is a continuing creative process, and over time this little book has been a joint effort with many. *The Book of Care* relates to the acronym for Compassionate Action Restoring Energy, and comes to you now with a warm heart and a big smile.

One morning the right thing was said at the right time and the process began. After the initial nudge, I called a dear friend who simply said to consider something small, perhaps a picture book with short statements of wisdom. Voila!

I began a popcorning process, creating a stack of notecards with thoughts and clever sayings. Synchronicity kept tumbling things out. I placed that little stack on an altar, and asked Dee Melendez, Mary Jane Adams, and Ruthe Barnudy, my golden goddesses, to enfold this creation with me.

Acknowledgements

Victor Hugo said, "All the forces in the world are not so powerful as an idea whose time has come." The birth of this book was like a little force that had been gathering momentum for a long time. The validation of the whole idea was swift and amazing. Within a short period of time, I had gathered a sufficient number of parts and pieces to create my book.

I am the scribe, but I give heartfelt and humble thanks to many others who assisted me along the way.

Stan Grindstaff is a magical editor, Linda Manzella is a wonderful graphic artist, and Laura Van Tyne and her team at Crystal Pointe Media are masterful at their craft. I give great thanks for my children and their children for their love and willing support of all of my endeavors. I honor my large extended family of friends, and my precious clients.

And I especially give thanks to those who walk this path with me now ~ Polly Martin, Bridgett Solley, Volker Brechbuhler, Andre Stevens-Thomas, and Jose Garcia.

Over many decades I have had innumerable mentors around the world who influenced me immensely, and I cherish the hours sitting at their feet.

For all things and good people ~ I give thanks!!!

Testimonials

"DeAnna has a wonderful command of coalescing the truth into delicious tidbits."
~ Andrew Bremness, M. D.

"DeAnna's messages express loving care in rich and meaningful ways."
~ Reverend Ruthe Barnudy, RScP

"As you read this book, open your eyes and breathe deeply. Just let it flow."
~ AS-T, Master Musician

"*The Book of CARE* is your walk through life's large grocery store, passing aisle by aisle, exploring the shelves of Authenticity, Beingness, Enlightenment, Gratitude and Karma. What's in store for you? Open the cover and step in..."

~ VB, Diplomat

"Thank you, Deanna, for always being there and for being an example of humility and integrity."
~ JG, Healer

"You are the epitome of grace and care."
~ BS, Business Entrepreneur

"DeAnna has been a facilitator of light when I was in a very dark place. Now I stand tall, with her beside me as inspiration."
~ SW, Milliner

"The Book of CARE shines a regenerative light to the vital areas of life. DeAnna's insight provides a high level of energy vibration, and her wisdom refocuses attention to appreciate the exuberant freedom and expansive joy found in every conscious moment.

"The Book of CARE could not come at a more critical time in our world. It is a simple, practical, and beautiful gift of grace and love that anyone can use to find peace and inspiration each and every day!"

~ JA, Private Client

"For many years I was controlled by a toxic world filled with toxic people. But in a short period of time after working with DeAnna, I gained knowledge, insight, and a new perspective bringing me a peace and bliss unknown before."

~JR, Private Client

Table of Contents

Energy 2

Being 4

Illumined 6

Beingness 8

Gratitude 10

Head vs Heart 12

Authenticity 14

I Am 16

Where My Thoughts Go My Energy Flows 18

Karma 20

Process & Procession 22

Radiance & Magnetization 24

Ego 26

Pause for Peace 28

Spiral	30
Ascension	32
Yin/Yang	34
Life Itself	36
Breath	38
"Be the Change that You Wish to See" – Gandhi	40
Co-Operative Venture	42
Presence	44
Alone ~ Add One 'l' ~ All One	46
Quietude	48
Life Is a Verb! Motion Is its Essence!	50
Resonance	52
Meet the Messenger	54

Energy

Invisible reality shaping everything on every level of all life. Energy is seemingly invisible but can be felt!

Being

I am a human *Being*.
I share physical substance and energetic essence
with *everyone*.
Humanness is the amazing physical
form and function.
Beingness is my Life force
energizing and activating my
anatomy and physiology.

Illumined

To be illumined is to relax
into the truth of my Beingness.
My Beingness enlivens my physicality
as I let my *Light* shine!

Beingness

Beingness lends potency to *Doingness*.
It is my right-brain function
of inclusiveness, empathy, tolerance
and compassion.
Rather than a *power over*, it is the quiet
power from within.

Gratitude

Life is my gift in each moment of living.
I ride the rhythm and grace of the *Breath of Life*.
Like the ebb and flow of the ocean...
breathing, inhaling and exhaling, is my gift.
Consciously, I appreciate all the dynamics
and provisions of Life Itself.
Maturity comes as I learn
to integrate the power of *Life's Process in Gratitude.*

Head vs Heart

My brain is a wonderful library of
stored information.
All data is useful in its place and when
the time is right.
Einstein pointed to his head, "This is not a leader."
He moved his hand to his heart.
"It is from here where you derive leadership."
My head alone is exclusive; my heart is inclusive.
It is much better to come from my Center
~*Wholeness, Harmony and Balance.*

Authenticity

I love relaxing into greater states of Inner Peace.
My assurance grows with a clear sense of Self.
My mind smiles and my heart sings
~ the *Song of Presence* prevails.

I Am

I Am an Ascended Master,
the Spirit that activates my human capacities.
I say, "I am" going to do something
hundreds of times a day.
I am going to call a friend,
going to walk barefoot,
going to the grocery store…
As I live in the consciousness of Being,
there is potency and power in my (*I Am*) Presence.
Friends, grass or beach, cashiers…
all feel the warmth of my genuineness.

Where My Thoughts Go My Energy Flows

Literally, where my thoughts are magnetized,
that is where my consciousness goes.
It takes honesty to catch myself
in a downward spiral,
and I can say, "Thus far, no further."
With that declaration, I can consciously
breathe and center.
I can turn negativity into positivity.
I can restore the natural, nourishing
restoration of the moment.
There is always potential in the flow of gratitude.

Karma

Karma returns to its Creator, (Me)
~ to be redeemed.
As painful as some things can be,
I allow them to rise.
I hold them in my hands, look at them, relax...
and shine my Light upon them.
This dissipates them, as
"Light dispels any darkness."
Yes, I am the Light!
This is the Age of Restoration.
This is a Renaissance bringing everything
back into intended Goodness.

Process & Procession

It takes courage
to honestly address my fears
with their memories.
When I take time to *process*,
I consciously release and join the *procession*,
moving forward in trust and faith.

Radiance & Magnetization

Through my eyes and every cell in my body
I radiate Universal Sun Energy.
The Laws of the Universe are pure and simple;
what I choose to project / radiate
will magnetize similar patterns back to me.
(What goes around comes around.)
I have the capacity to restore fragmentation
with balance
by *pausing for peace.*

Ego

My ego-mind is a bully trying to
sway me off balance.
The Law of the Circle
is a barometer for my Radiance and Magnetization.
We are of God-Parent heritage
and when my ego takes over
I am Edging God Out.
(acronym EGO)

Pause for Peace

This is my invitation to catch myself caringly.
Consciously I breathe deeply
to increase and celebrate reconnection.
I release chaos
endowing myself with perfection of
~Harmony and Balance.

Spiral

All of nature grows in a spiral design.
The ascending energy of Life
allows my consciousness to lift up and up.
I lift up out of time and space
and the pull of gravity.
Life is a verb and I am in motion!
Let me move with the *Grace of Restoration*.

Ascension

Everything I touch is raised in consciousness
here and now.
I love exploring the Lightness of Being,
the wonder of Light Service,
enjoying privileges of physical freedom,
my gratitude rising *Buoyant and Free.*

Yin/Yang

In perfect harmony and balance…
Divine Feminine and Divine Masculine.
Complete.
Unified.

Life Itself

Life is all of creation on every level...
the entirety of time.
Before philosophies and religions, there was Life.
Life's energy has been *life-ing*
everything all along...
delivered by the breath.

Breath

Breath is the gift of Life Itself,
energy given freely, unconditionally, lovingly.

"Be the Change That You Wish to See"
~ *Gandhi*

I can be *at cause*
rather than being *at the effect*
of everything around me.
It is my choice to align myself,
and to come from a place of inner stability.
I can be a *Victor*
rather than a
poor-me-ain't-it-awful
victim all the time.

Co-Operative Venture

*There is nothing so powerful as gentleness;
there is nothing so gentle as pure power.*
~ 14th Century Couplet

I am a victorious expression of Life.
I consciously engage and share in all of Life's activity.
My intention springs *from Cause*
as I welcome any and all circumstances.

Presence

The radiance of my truth
is a *Being* of Light
having a human experience...
seemingly invisible energy
permeates and surrounds my physical form.

Alone ~ Add One 'l' ~ All One

In reality
I am never alone
when I reside in the whole truth
of who I Am.
Aloneness and separation
are of a fearful human ego.

Quietude

My restful focus is in the *Silence* of meditation.
I *take time to take time* to consciously restore.
It's as close as one conscious breath…
Sigh…

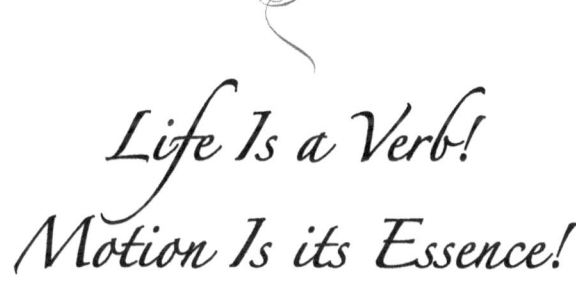

Life Is a Verb!
Motion Is its Essence!

Everything in the Universe is of Life's energy
always moving and in motion.
Everything affects everything.
I am mindful of enjoying
the *Grace* of the *Dance*.

Resonance

Sounds, tones, senses relating to one another.
As an instrument in an orchestra,
I bring my unique wave or frequency
to each situation.
I yearn to resonate with all.
I love to be in harmony with the entire orchestra!

Meet the Messenger

I have enjoyed many roles: wife, mother, grandmother, businesswoman, facilitator, writer and poet, mentor, catalyst, and activist—always looking for a fresh path to resolution. I have shared closely in the profound change, healing, and restoration of those responsive to my tutelage and guidance.

> Recently, I was honored by this tribute:
> "Wisdom Weaver."

I have also vaulted many emotional and physical hurdles. But, alas, living, like a lovely lyrical poem, is energy in motion. And in spite of some upsets, I dance a joyful jig. My motto is always, "Life is a verb, *motion is its essence*." It's a matter of trusting the wholeness, where the harvest is always abundant.

My life is dedicated to fostering change in myself and in the larger body of humanity. This glorious journey to inner peace begins with a tranquil heart.

> Most Gratefully,
> *DeAnna LoCoco*

To learn more about DeAnna and her work, please visit:
www.letenergytransform.com

www.ingramcontent.com/pod-product-compliance
Lightning Source LLC
Chambersburg PA
CBHW051714040426
42446CB00008B/887